MW01251420

PROPERTY OF
ST. JOHN AMBULANCE
THERAPY DOG DIVISION

Working As A Therapy Dog; Observations and tips from an experienced therapy dog. Copyright © 2002 by Lorna Stanart. All rights reserved. No part of this book may be reproduced in any form or by any electronic or mechanical means including information storage and retrieval systems without permission in writing from the publisher, except by a reviewer, who may quote brief passages in a review. Published by Hispen Books, P.O. Box 2394, Palm Springs, California 92263.

To order additional copies of this book visit www.hispenbooks.com or check your local bookstore.

1st Edition

ISBN 0-9728067-0-9

Library of Congress Control Number: 2003103736

Edited by Mary Anna King
Cover photo by Wendy Victor
Cover design by Scott Guptill
Printed by Loma Linda University Printing Services

PROPERTY OF
ST. JOHN AMBULANCE
THERAPY DOG DIVISION

Working As A Therapy Dog

Observations and tips from an experienced therapy dog

by Breeze Stanart

as told to my owner,

Lorna Stanart

Thank you to my husband, Richard, for always encouraging me in this project.

Thank you to Ann Whitton for getting me started in Animal Assisted Therapy and for her wisdom in dog training and canine behavior.

Chapter Outline
&
Table of Contents

Chapter 1
Beginnings

My story could have turned out the same if I'd started life living on the streets, but as it happened, I was born to loving, pedigree parents. My full name is Mistry's Summer Breeze, but you can call me Breeze. My humans said they named me that because I was "as welcome as a summer breeze" when they brought me home to live with them in the Southern California desert area.

Yes, I was blessed to have humans who waited on a waiting list until I was born, but many of my well qualified co-workers haven't even known their Dad's name, let alone had humans to feed and love them. Their "rags to riches" stories have come *not* from the soft beds and doggie biscuits they've received after being rescued from the pound, but rather, the riches are those "gems of joy" that they have *given* to humans through their eventual work as therapy dogs.

My parents were both Great Pyrenees dogs. Great Pyrenees were bred for guarding livestock, like sheep or goats. We are calm, peaceful dogs who thoughtfully survey situations and make our own decisions on how best to respond. We would be very gentle with young lambs born in the pasture with us. We are protectors at heart. Our job as a livestock guardian dog would not be to run around the mountainside herding the flock at the shepherd's command. A herding dog would do that job. We would stand guard, watching over our flock, watching for any dangerous intruders coming near. Only a foolish wolf, coyote or bear would come around our flock with a few Pyrs on the job.

I am a giant dog. Boys, like me, usually weigh between 100 to 125 lbs. I have long white fur and many 'feathers' of long white fur down the backs of my legs and on my tail. My tail has a shepherd's crook at the end. I have a thick ruff of fur around my neck. Some people think it makes me look like a lion, but I am really as gentle as a lamb. I have a patch of gray over one eye and gray fur on my ears.

I work as a therapy dog --- Animal Assisted Therapy is their fancy title for it, but we dogs just call it Love.

Chapter 2
Early Training

My training began at the age of 3 months. It was fun to try to gnaw on the leash while my human "Mom" tried to be serious. I soon learned how to trot along by her side, sneaking a quick nip at the leash whenever possible.

Me, age 9 weeks

If I'd have known how happy Mom would get when I learned to sit, I'd have done it sooner. It was easy, once I knew what she wanted me to do.

By about 4 months of age I had learned to heel and sit well enough to start going on outings. That was really fun. Mom would take me to different stores. We would wait outside the store and lots of friendly humans would pet me - some big people and some little ones. I especially liked the little ones. They always smelled so interesting. I was as tall as most children under 5 years of age now. I could sniff their cheek or their ear and they'd giggle. They looked kind of topply, so I never pushed against them. Some looked like they might fall over if I did. I loved it when they'd touch my fur. I found out it made *them* smile too.

We were always going to new stores and meeting new people. It was fun. I didn't understand then, that Mom was taking me there for part of my training to be a therapy dog, but now that I'm older, I have seen several dogs fail to qualify to be a therapy dog because they were so nervous being in a strange place and having strangers touch them and talk to them during their testing.

These outings to stores with Mom continued once a week for several months until I was about 8 or 10 months old. The outings were fun and never seemed like work.

During this time, at home, I learned the words "down", "come", "stay" and "housey" (my crate) ... some better than others. I learned that "O.K. Puppy" meant the lesson was over for that day. Most days Mom and I spent 10 to 15 minutes working on my studies. Most of it was easy.

What was much more difficult was learning what I was allowed to chew on and what made Mom yell when I chewed on it. Take for instance, one afternoon when I was laying in the den, happily gnawing on my chew bone. I was thoroughly enjoying myself and Mom was watching TV and listening to me chew on my bone. It was quite by accident, that the bone rolled over a few inches to the wall and I found out that the corner of the den wall was nice and chewy too! I don't know why Mom was so upset. The hole in the corner of the wall was only about 3 inches big! That was the day I found out that it wasn't O.K. to chew on *that* wall. I did try tasting a few other walls in our home over the next few months. Funny thing ... I always heard the same angry sounds come out of Mom when I did. But I was beginning to see a pattern ...

Where to potty also took some time for me to figure out. When you're a 60 lb. 6 month old puppy, you can't hide it when 'Niagara Falls' happens in the living room. Mom has very good hearing, too. She was always sweeter about correcting my mistakes when she heard me do it, rather than having her sock find it at a later time.

By the time I was about a year old, I had not had any potty accidents in the house for a long time. My temperament and training had produced behavior which would allow me to qualify to begin my work as a therapy dog.

Chapter 3
My Purpose

It's important for a therapy dog to wait by his handler's side until the patient he's visiting invites him to approach. Can you believe, some patients don't like dogs? So I stand calmly and quietly by my Mom's left leg, watching and waiting for the "go see" hand signal from Mom. It's a slow hand motion made by her left hand, at my eye level, where I can see it. Her flat hand, fingers together, sweeps gently in the direction of the patient and I know I may step forward to get petted. This is, of course, my favorite of all! Since I have never tried to jump on people, I am allowed the freedom to stand next to the patient in whatever position he and I find most comfortable. Mom still holds the end of the leash, but she moves

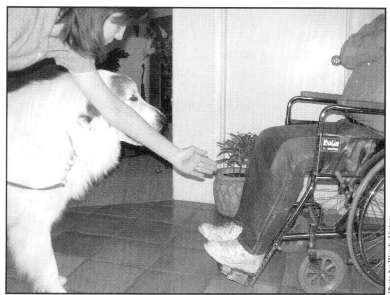

The "go see" hand signal

away to the end of the 6 foot leash and stands, without talking, allowing my ministry to begin.

God has given me the gift of patience. I will stand with one patient for as long as 15 minutes without moving. If I sense that their touch is quite feeble, I wait for as long as it takes for each stroke that they pet me. If their touch is vigorous, I'll often hug my side toward their chest while they sit in their wheelchair.

A special connection takes place between the patient and me at that point. They feel my soft fur, yes, but more than that, they feel my breathing, my peace. The essence of my being meets theirs and for a time we just *are* .... This is the time when depression and loneliness lift off the patient. The blanket of peace that I bring to them, wraps also around them, as we are together.

What great price can be put on the value of a hug? In some facilities I visit, the staff are legally forbidden to touch or hug the patients, but we therapy dogs can! This is especially true in some psychiatric facilities. I give my warm affection to a patient for a few minutes, but the love that comes with it lasts much longer.

Chapter 4
The Boy Jason

There was a boy named Jason, who lived with 5 other physically and mentally challenged teenagers in a special home. I visited them twice a month for 2 years. Jason could walk on his own with the help of leg braces. He was about 16 years old. The first time I came to visit him, my Mom asked him if he would like to walk me around inside the home. Jason happily accepted. But as soon as my 6 foot leash was in his hand, Jason began swinging the leash around wildly, as if turning a jump rope. I had no idea what *that* signal was, so I figured the best thing to do was to sit. "Oh Mom! What does this mean?" my eyes asked her. She smiled at me and nodded her head in silence. I knew that meant that it was O.K. for me to walk with Jason. Mom tied a big knot in my leash, shortening it to about 1 foot in length. And although Jason's two hands continued to swing around spastically during our walk together, that helped a lot. Mom walked a step behind us as Jason walked me from room to room in the house, telling me all about each room. From time to time, I'd look over my shoulder to check if Mom was still with us. Her smile and nod of reassurance was all I needed to continue. When we got to his room, he showed me some of his special toys, which I sniffed with mild interest. When Jason sat on the edge of his bed, Mom pried the leash out of his hand so that Jason could focus more on me. I liked Jason and I hugged the side of my body to his chest as he sat on the edge of his bed.

Since Jason had difficulty in forming sentences, when he *did* formulate a sentence he would always say it 3 times. He told my Mom, "You sit down." "You sit down." "You sit down." so she sat on the edge of the bed a few feet away. I know she was always watching over me to be sure that Jason never hurt me, but she has a sneaky way of watching out of the corner of her eye, without meeting eyes with me. Dogs like me, with obedience training, will often look to their handler for approval, to make sure they are doing what the handler wants. But if the handler holds their gaze, the dog will continue their connection with the handler instead of relating to the patient. Mom usually looks at the floor while I'm with someone. I know she can see everything that's going on between the patient and me with her peripheral vision.

As you might guess, I was very surprised, when one day Jason said, "Breeze's nose" and the next thing I knew his slender finger was up my nose. I didn't move a muscle, but craned my eyes toward Mom. My expression saying, "Oh Mom! What about this? He's got his finger up my nose!" The second "Breeze's nose" also made it up my nose before Mom could move into action. She moved the boy's hand before he repeated his words and actions the third time. She put Jason's hand on my back and said, "How about Breeze's back?" I knew Jason meant me no harm, but it felt weird. I shrugged it off and remained lying on the mat with him for the rest of our time together.

During our visits over those 2 years, Jason and I had many cuddles and smiles together. Sometimes we would lie together on a mat in the living room. After about 8 months of visits, we witnessed a tremendous change in Jason's behavior. He and I were lying on the mat cuddled up together for about 20 minutes. We both were lying on our side. My back was snuggled against Jason's stomach. When our visiting time was over, my Mom said to the Physical Therapist, "Which one should we wake up first, Jason or Breeze?". Neither of us had moved for the past 15 minutes and we both had our backs to them. The Physical Therapist walked around and looked at Jason's face. To her absolute amazement, Jason's eyes were open!!! Prior to this day, the only way Jason could be that still was if he was sleeping, but that wasn't the case. He was just chillin' with his friend, Breeze.

Chapter 5
Something's Afoot

I worked for almost 2 years on a hospital sub-acute ward, just to be there for one special day. As I left a patient's room, I saw a man in his fifties beckoning me with his arm to come to his son's room. His son was about 25 years old and was in bed, kicking and swinging his arms. The Rehab Therapist (RT) told us that the young man had suffered a very recent head injury. She also told us that he was in the agitated phase of coma, in which his arms and legs thrashed uncontrollably. She wasn't sure that he knew his Dad was there by his bedside. None of us were sure he understood when his Dad told him in Spanish that a large dog was here to visit him.

My co-worker, a Toy Poodle, could take no part in ministering to *this* patient. It was simply too dangerous for the little dog.

There were large pads strapped to the man's hands for his protection. They could have been removed, but his arms were moving about so wildly that my Mom thought it best to find some other approach. While we stood by the bed, my Mom saw that when the patient kicked, the flat, bottom of his foot would always slam against the metal upright end of the bed. The patient was barefoot.

Mom gave me the "go see" hand signal, directing me to stand on all fours at the foot of the bed. I took my place and leaned my side against the metal foot of the bed. I heard Mom say to the RT, "Maybe he can reach the dog with his toes." The RT gently stretched the man's toes forward, over the end of the bed and then removed her hand. I felt his toes touch the fur on my back, then the toes stopped. They moved a little more, then stopped again. Then the toes nestled down in my fur and stopped moving again. It was as if the toes were pausing to comprehend what they were touching. Deep in my long hair, the toes rested. The man's whole body rested .... then WHAM! a strong kick! The man's full, flat foot landed against the foot of the bed. I felt the strong vibration through the metal footboard against which I was leaning. I took one side-step away from the foot of the bed and looked up at Mom. She smiled and nodded at me. She whispered "It's O.K. boy". I always like it when she talks to me like that. Then I followed her hand signal to walk in a circle. I was back in position, standing at the foot of the bed again. I looked at Mom, then leaned my side against the metal foot of the bed once again, lowered my head and waited. Again came the friendly toes. They felt good nestling in my fur and exploring around my back. I could feel the patient's whole body relax when the toes snuggled the warm skin deep under my fur. The RT said, "It's relaxing him." The spasms had stopped, even if only for a few seconds. We knew that touching me made a connection inside this man's mind with something familiar. His brain was working hard to recognize and enjoy a dog - not his own dog, but a familiar companion, a special part of his life at home.

WHAM! and again the foot struck the end of the bed. Again I took one step to the side. Again Mom patted my head, spoke gently to me, and guided me back into position. We did this over and over, perhaps 5 or 6 times. Although I didn't like the sound of the foot slamming against the end of the bed or the vibration against my side, I was never in any danger of being kicked. The man's full leg extension was needed for him to reach to pet me with his toes pointed. It was not possible for him to reach me with his full foot. And you know, I trust my Mom. If she asked me to stand there, then it must be O.K. I know she would never put me in a position to get hurt. I forgave the foot each time it kicked and I walked in a circle back into position to work some more.

As we began to walk out of the man's room, his Dad followed us. He shook my Mom's hand as he thanked her in Spanish several times. Then he held her hand in both of his, as he looked into her

12

eyes. His eyes had an expression of new hope. He had seen his son respond to me.

In the weeks that followed, we always looked for this man on the unit. In one of our later visits, with his Dad on one side and the RT on the other, they helped him to sit up in bed to pet me. Then the patient reached out and grabbed his own ankle, pulling it into a cross-legged position to steady himself. I stayed with him as he petted my back and head with his hands. He was clumsy, but neither he nor I minded. We just wanted to spend some time together.

After that session, the RT explained to us how critically important it is to get the brain to focus on something after a head injury. They sometimes use flash cards or brightly colored toys to get the patient's attention but these things are not as interesting to a patient who is a dog lover. This man *wanted* to focus on me and positioned himself to pet me. It probably didn't even seem like work to him. Just a furry friend coming to visit.

This young man had been kicked in the head by his horse. Although he had been injured by one of his own animals, the visits from *another* animal had helped in some ways with the miraculous healing taking place in his body and mind. His progress was steady and then he was transferred to another facility to continue his recovery.

Chapter 6
Numerous Maneuvers

My work in the Sub-Acute Ward often required that we be creative in maneuvering our way around the patients. All of them had tracheotomy tubes. Many of them were in various stages of coma. Some were alert but their arms and hands were so atrophied that they could not reach out to pet us.

One time we noticed that a female patient was raising and lowering her stiffened leg repeatedly when a dog came near her. When the Rehab Therapist took her sock off, the lady stroked my fur with her atrophied foot. She smiled at me while she stroked me. I had to stand very still and not lean against her leg.

Sometimes a patient would get so excited to see us that their arm movements would knock their own trachea tube off. Any time that would happen, an alarm would go off until the nurse standing with us would re-attach it. The alarms and all the other machinery noises never bothered my co-worker or me, but some dogs take some time to get used to the sounds of the equipment. The best thing their owner can do is to watch their dog for signs of stress. If they see that the dog gets too worried, they should take the dog into the hallway to relax a minute and then go back into the patient's room. If the owner talks to the dog in a cheerful, relaxed way, it will rub off on the therapy dog. If the owner gets worried or sympathizes with the dog too much, it will make the dog much more nervous about the situation.

The more a dog can say, "been there, done that", before starting work as a therapy dog, the better. Being exposed in small increments to noises like shopping carts clamoring together, a public toilet flushing, or various squeaks and squeals of the big world is easiest when a potential therapy dog is in puppyhood, but can be started at any time in a dog's life. I was walking down the hospital corridor with my Mom and my co-worker (a Toy Poodle named Mischa) and his Mom one day, when a maintenance man started drilling a hole in the wall. Mischa and I just shrugged our shoulders and kept on walking - no big deal. It's also good if you're used to elevators and automatic doors.

It's often much easier for a person in a wheelchair to reach to pet a dog if the dog is sitting on the floor *beside* his/her wheelchair instead of in front of him/her.

Mischa could get in bed and lay down next to some of the patients whose injuries allowed it. One lady, who had been in a car accident, had so many pins and plates in her body, there was no place to even put the little dog, but his owner held him and moved one of his front paws to stroke the lady's skin with the back of Mischa's wrist. The patient enjoyed that and said that Mischa's visit helped her to forget for a few minutes that she was in the hospital. It was a welcome break from the reality of her pain and trauma.

I have had to duck under plastic tubing sometimes in order to get close enough for a patient to touch me. There I stand, with my head lowered, as I enjoy their slow and featherlike touch. I ignore the urinary catheter that hangs nearby because I know it would embarrass the patient if I sniffed it. I pay no attention to I.V. tubes or pulse meters either because I have been taught the "leave it" command for sanitary reasons. I am there to meet the person behind all those tubes and machines.

Mom has sometimes used the plumes of my tail to stroke an atrophied patient. It gives an extra 2 feet of length with which to reach someone in bed. I must tell you, I'm not so keen on that maneuver. It feels weird. But Beau, another co-worker with me on Sub-Acute, tolerates it very well. He is a Golden Retriever/Great Pyrenees Mix and a marvelous therapy dog. His friendliness and tranquility touch the patients even if his fur can't reach them. Sometimes Beau's Mom lifts his front legs off the ground so he's standing on his back legs while she holds his front paws in her hands. That way the patient who is staring straight ahead or upwards can get a glimpse of his beautiful face and then they'll lower their gaze to look at him once they see that he's there. I've seen Beau put a front paw on the bed rail to give his Mom a hand with this maneuver.

And then there's Faith. Faith is a Golden Retriever who has developed a maneuver of her own which comes in very handy in her work in an adult Oncology Ward. Of course a therapy dog is not allowed to jump up on a bed because of the danger of hurting a patient. Small dogs are lifted by their owners and placed on the bed where the nurse indicates. Then a "down - stay" hand signal assures that a small dog will stay still. But Faith is a rather large dog who her owner cannot lift. So Faith's approach is this: She walks quietly up to the patient's bed and greets them while they pat her head. This initial meeting tells Faith how she is received by the patient. Faith can certainly recognize a true dog lover, and when she meets one, she crawls, moving her front feet slowly up the side of the bed, bit by bit. With each crawling movement she advances about 3 or 4 inches until her front paws are lying on the bed and her head is often in the patient's lap. What joy she brings to the patients!

Auggie is a Golden Retriever with immense patience and gentleness. When a person sits or lies down on the carpet next to him, he lies down and lets time fade away. He enjoys being close *that* way.

So you see, sometimes we dogs and our owners have to be creative in finding ways to reach out to the people we visit.

Chapter 7
Furry Tranquilizer

One ward of my hospital work where I most often see immediate results is in the Psychiatric Ward. The adult men and women I visit there are commonly admitted because of depression, substance abuse recovery, or a chemical imbalance in their brain. The patients must not be combative or violent towards humans or animals to be allowed into a session with a therapy dog. My co-worker and I move from person to person, staying with each individual for as long as they want. The patients see us and come out of their rooms. If they are playing cards or watching TV, we visit them while they do so. We make our rounds in the living room-like setting, making sure we don't miss anyone. We <u>do</u> keep track of that, you know. I always know if there's a person in the room who has not yet petted me. I walk towards them, stop, and look at them, waiting for their outstretched hand or the "go see" hand signal from Mom. I'm careful not to leave anyone out.

The dogs bring some of the outside world into the unit and rekindle a desire in the patients to be well. Recently, near the end of our one-hour stay, a lady in her late 50's said to my Mom, "Look at the smiles in this place now! This is the first time today I've seen anyone smile. It just makes my heart full of joy that you have come here today with your dog. This is better than a hundred pills!"

One day as a male patient was rubbing my head, I felt very content and was enjoying the massage he was giving me. A lady patient, watching, told my Mom, "Breeze will leave here happy today!" My Mom replied, "Oh he always leaves here happy. You guys treat him so nicely when he comes to visit." I could tell by the lady patient's voice that it had made *her* happy to see *me* happy.

Studies have shown that petting an animal lowers blood pressure. I don't know all the facts, but I know what I see. Sometimes near the end of our hour, my doggie co-worker and I will lie down on the carpet and take a nap. My Mom has told me that she has frequently seen patients sit and watch us sleep. Even watching us sleep is calming to them. For this reason, my Mom never cuts the session off before the full hour even if the people in the room have all petted us as much as they want.

Photo by Wendy Victor

We get many offers from patients in the Psyche Ward to spend the night. They probably miss their own dog sleeping with them in bed. But we say our "good-byes" until the next time when we'll be back in 2 weeks.

Chapter 8
Tricks

Some of us have learned tricks which we like to perform for the people we visit. I have seen dogs do a "high five" with their paw on cue from their owner. I have seen them "shake" hands/paws too. The most important thing with either of these tricks is that the dog only does them on command. Otherwise a dog might simply be trying to shake hands and inadvertently clobber a patient. Some of us have really big feet.

My trick is to "give a hug". This is very popular with the psychiatric patients because they are able to kneel on the floor to get in position. When my Mom taps the patient's right shoulder, I plunk my big head on their shoulder and snuggle my head to their neck. Oh how the patients love my hugs!

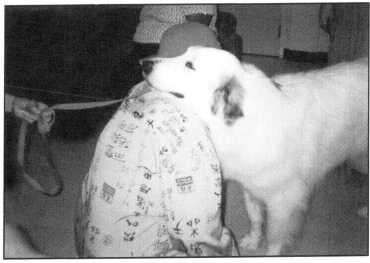

"give a hug"

I have heard that my predecessor, Rex, used to do an ear trick. When my Mom used to say "ears up ... ears down ... ears up ... ears down" Rex would raise and lower his ears. He was a Terrier/Whippet mix and had good ears for that trick. The patients really got a kick out of it.

Tricks are good because they strengthen the relationship between the therapy dog and his or her owner. A strong bond there makes for a confident therapy dog. Our tricks never include barking or other vocalizations. That would be too startling for the other people in the facility. Tricks like "roll over" or even "sit" and "down" with hand signals are enjoyed by the people too. We don't do tricks every time we go to visit, but sometimes they're just the thing to help spread some smiles.

Chapter 9
A Dog's Day Off

Two weeks after my bath, after I have made all four of my visits for the month, I have the next two weeks to just be a dog.

I live on a 5 acre ranch with 3 humans; my "Mom" and "Dad" and my little boy, Lionel, who is my very good friend. He is 8 years old. Mom and Dad work at home, so we have them here most days.

Breeze with Lionel

I have 2 other dogs to play with at home. Kasheena is a girl Great Pyrenees who is also a therapy dog. She was 4 years old when she came to live with us. Her previous family used to let her jump up on them to greet them. Her front paws could easily rest on an adult human's shoulders while she would welcome them home. So Kasheena needed to learn to greet people without jumping up before starting her work as a therapy dog. It took a full year before she was completely reliable to not jump on people. Now Dad has been taking her to work at a Retirement Home for over a year. She is now 6 years old. Two years older than me. We Pyrs are nocturnal dogs, so Kasheena and I have a blast running, playing and patrolling the 5 acres all night long, every night. We are also making sure our family is safe. Playful Pyrs will often rear up on their back legs and body slam each other, imitating in play how they would really take down a predator, if necessary. We only play this way with other Pyrs. Kasheena and I are great playmates.

Kasheena with Lionel

Alex is our new puppy. He's a 6 month old Sheltie and he's just beginning his studies. Some day he'll make a fine therapy dog. He has a calm demeanor, he is loving to humans, and he shows an amazing ability for self control in his early obedience lessons. The guy is as quick as a whip! He's in his formative months, so sometimes during his naps Mom will say, "Alex, come". Without even a stretch, he prances over to her for a cuddle. After a minute of patting him, Mom goes back into her office and Alex goes back to his nap. This is known to build the little tyke's confidence and his trust in his family of humans. He is learning that he <u>will</u> be called on for a cuddle. He is also learning that Mom is the "lead dog" in our pack when it comes to dog training. Also, that she loves him and that she is kind and cuddly with him. He is also learning that he doesn't have to get frantic about asking for attention by jumping and barking, and the like. When he least expects it, he will be called on for a little lovin'. All that from being called to "come" while he's sleeping! I remember those wake-up lessons when I was Alex's age. I understand them more now than I did then. At 4 years old now, I just raise my eyebrow and open one eye while I remain sprawled out on the living room couch because the lessons are not for me now. They're for my pal, Al. Alex and I love to romp and play together in the mornings and evenings. I pretend he has knocked me down and then I let him pull the hair around my neck and on my tummy and skip around me in circles. The only days we're not allowed to play together are the 3 days after my bath.

Then there are those cats. There are 2 of them; Basil and Goldie. They are 4 years old and in the prime of life. Dogs are never allowed to chase cats. I learned that rule early. Even when the cats are flying through the house, jumping over the fur-

Alex, age 3 months

niture and tearing from one room to another while playing together in the evening. Dogs are not allowed to run in the house. How is that fair? Cats are allowed to sleep anywhere they want. Even in the office next to the fax machine. (Goldie's favorite place) Dogs aren't allowed to cross the threshold to the office. Who made up these rules anyway? I know our big dog feet have something to do with important paperwork in the office or something like that. Cats are O.K. I guess, but they're not really much fun. Oh, and for any dogs reading this, I should warn you that they *do* have claws and they're not afraid to use them!

I also live with 2 horses on our ranch. Horses are like <u>really</u> big dogs. Kasheena and I don't usually go inside their corrals, but we always get a drink from their automatic waterers. Add a little sand and horse manure dust to a white dog's coat and you'll know why I get a bath before going to work at a hospital or nursing home.

We also have a few hens and a goat. I don't pay attention to them really. They're just there in their pen. "Live and let live" I say. We don't really have anything in common.

Sometimes the little boy and I snuggle in his big double bed together. I'm glad they bought him a big bed so there's enough room for

Breeze resting his head on Lionel. Kasheena lying nearby.

him and me and usually one cat. I love to play "tag" and "hide-and-go-chase-ya" with the little boy. I've never really understood why some dogs like to play "ball". It does nothing for me. (or most Pyrs, as a matter of fact) Mostly I just like to "hang" with my little boy, Lionel. Whether I'm lying down on a mound of sand watching him play in his mud puddle or whether I follow him across the 40 foot suspension bridge into his fort, I like to be where he is.

Hangin' around the house. The little boy made us comfortable. Kasheena looks like she's listening to music, but her tape player was not turned on.

It's a good life on the ranch. I lift my head up from the couch when I smell lunch cooking for my Mom and Dad. I walk over to the counter where my bowl is kept and I look at my bowl of dog kibble. The counter is at my eye level. I have trained my humans to know that means I want them to set my bowl down so I can eat. Even though I'm tall enough to help myself, I don't, because that wouldn't be polite, would it? I lie down and munch some kibble. (I eat 4 times a day.) Then I hop back up on the couch for the afternoon until the little boy gets home from school. Yes, life is good on the ranch.

Chapter 10
The Touch That Sees

I remember my first day on the job. It was at a nursing home. My Mom and I were greeted in the lobby by about 6 of the residents who were sitting in their wheelchairs waiting for "dog day". When they saw me, they were so excited! They ooh-ed and aah-ed and asked many, many questions about me. My Mom chose one resident who was clapping her hands and saying "Here, boy!" and gave me the "go see" hand signal towards her. I walked over to her with a lazy swish of my tail. She was smiling and laughing and talking to me as she patted me. For such a little lady she could really give a dog a good rub-down. I thoroughly enjoyed it.

My Mom answered everyone's questions about my name, my breed and how much I eat. She never tires of answering these questions over and over as we make our way through a facility. Although my Mom's role is not to initiate conversation with the people we visit, she politely gives brief answers to their questions. Often nursing home residents are without a pet dog for the first time in many, many years and they cherish the minutes they can spend with a dog. They want to interact with the dog, not the dog owner. So the dog owner stays at the end of the leash and waits quietly for their visit to be over.

After spending some time with each of the people in the lobby, we slowly started to make our way down the hallways and into the bedrooms of the nursing home residents. At each bedroom doorway we would stop at the threshold and my Mom would say, "Hello. Would you like to pet the dog?" She sometimes added hand gestures if the person was really hard of hearing.

I was looking over my shoulder from time to time during the hour visit, wondering when someone was going to vaccinate me! After all, we had never done anything like this before and the medical smells in the nursing home did remind me of a vet's office.

One little lady who was looking forward to the dogs coming to visit that day, had saved me the chicken out of her sandwich. My Mom thanked her for her thoughtfulness and told her, "He only eats dog food." The lady understood and agreed not to feed it to me. Hey, nobody asked me! I would have been willing to make an exception this one time, but my Mom knew that adding food treats to our visits would change my focus from the people to the food.

We met many friendly folk that day. One man told me that it was the first time in 50 years that he didn't have a dog. A lady whispered to me that she likes dogs better than people. She always had Samoyeds, so my white coat reminded her of the fond memories of her own pets.

We stopped at a bedroom doorway where inside we saw 3 beds. One man was standing a few feet away from us, next to his bed and a second man was sitting on the edge of the center bed. My Mom spoke to the closer man first. "Hello. Would you like to pet the dog?" she said. He said "yes", patted me on the top of my head twice, and said, "thank you". As we turned our attention to the second man, who was sitting on his bed, the first man said, "He doesn't want to pet the dog. He's blind." My Mom said, "It doesn't matter if he's blind." We stood about 3 feet in front of the blind man. My Mom asked her usual question; "There's a dog here to visit you. Would you like to pet him?" The man gave no response. Thinking he might be hard of hearing, she asked again, more loudly. Still no response. The man remained sitting on the edge of his bed, his eyelids closed. At that point, my Mom must have guessed that the man could not understand English, but that he'd like to pet me if he knew I was there. My Mom gave me the "go see" hand signal. I stepped forward and sniffed the man's hand. Then, as my Mom said "hello" again, I placed my face on the man's folded hands. A smile lit up the man's face as he lovingly patted my head. My really big head! Without saying a word, the man tapped me lightly all over my head. A broad smile still on his face, his eye-lids still closed, he continued his light tapping movements all around my neck. Then, while one hand remained on my face, the other tapped it's way down my back ... all the way down my back ... even farther down my back. (It's a long way to my tail, you know.) With his eyebrows raised in surprise, and joy all over his face, the man finally reached my tail and gave a little chuckle. He never said a word that day of our first visit, but I stayed with him for more than 15 minutes. He and I instantly became friends that day. There was a warmth that we shared that I can only describe as instant friendship. Any time the man took his hands off of me, I would gently plunk my face in his hands again or snuggle his knee to show him that I wanted his touch. The man would laugh each time I did these things. This man was definitely a "dog person" and he was asking me (by stopping his petting) to show him if I want-ed his petting or if I wanted to leave. Both he and I wanted to be together and it was clear to both of us. Mom never said a word either that day. Words were not necessary. But I know I saw a lit-tle tear of joy trickle down Mom's cheek as she watched us together.

When we returned to the same nursing home 2 weeks later, I was especially looking forward to visiting the blind man, who we later came to know as Pasquale. When we got to his room, he was again sitting on the edge of his bed. My Mom said, "hello" so as not to startle him as I walked over to him. When I placed my head in his hands, much to our surprise, he said, "My friend! My friend!" He said nothing more that visit, but his loving hands caressed me and communicated with me as we interacted together again that day. I know that as a therapy dog I'm supposed to like everybody, and almost always do, but I must say that I especially liked Pasquale.

I visited Pasquale (and the other residents at that nursing home) twice a month for about 6 months. On rare occasions, a Spanish speaking nurse would be in the room when we arrived and she and Pasquale would talk about me. She would translate his questions from Spanish and she would tell him things he wanted to know about me, like my age and my breed. Then one day he wasn't there. Mom asked at the nurse's station about him and we were told that his family had decided to take care of him at home. So he was back at home with his own 6 dogs. I was happy for him, but I missed my friend.

Chapter 11
Don't Judge a Book ...

In hospitals, a staff member should always escort you from bed to bed, but in nursing homes, you are usually free to visit from room to room on your own. It's possible that your human could misjudge a nursing home resident's interest in petting a dog if he/she is not sensitive to small indicators. My Mom made that kind of mistake once, and I'll tell you about it.

There was a man who was always in his wheelchair in the hallway of the nursing home where we visited. My Mom always passed by him without asking him if he wanted to pet me. The man's tongue always hung out of his mouth. His eyes were crossed, and he never spoke. My Mom thought he was too "out of it" to want to pet me. We'll call him Frank.

But one day, after getting a nice, slow massage from another man in the hallway, I took two steps and I was standing next to Frank's wheelchair. Both of Frank's hands were on my back in an instant. He began laughing out loud and rubbing me vigorously. His head swung from side to side as he laughed and laughed. Boy, did this man know how to give a dog a rub-down! What a wonderful massage he gave me! Although his hand movements were sort of awkward, his touch was kind. Mom was sure surprised and she felt badly for skipping Frank so many times before. After that we realized that if a resident is in the hallway or the recreation room, it's probably because the staff knows that he/she will enjoy the visit and respond to the activities. We never skipped Frank again.

Chapter 12
Renee

Renee is a girl in her early twenties who loves animals. Before the car accident that left her mentally impaired and in a wheelchair, she used to ride horses and loved to play with her dogs.

Renee and Breeze

Every time I came to see Renee she would hug me and kiss me on the top of the head. I found out that she had a pretty strong left arm! She'd wrap her arm around my neck and pull me towards her. I knew she only wanted to get close to me, but it was uncomfortable for me to be pulled tightly and squeezed against her wheelchair. Her gentle kiss on the top of my head was my reward for tolerating the awkward position. We had to find a better way to get close.

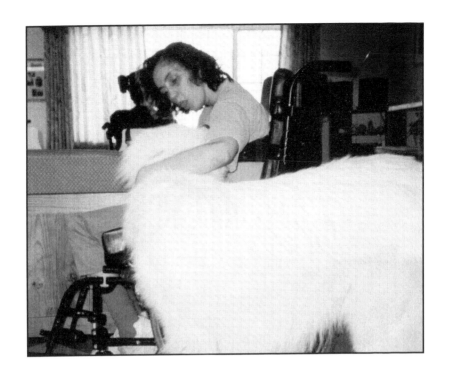

It happened one day, through a blessing in disguise, that the solution was discovered. When we came for our scheduled visit, we were told that Renee was just getting over the flu and was in her bed. The staff showed Renee her YES / NO board so that she could answer if she wanted to see me that day or not. She pointed to YES. I walked over to her where she lay in her twin size bed and she reached through the bed rails to pat me. That's when the idea hit us. My Mom said to the staff that perhaps I could lie down next to Renee in her bed. It would be a terrific opportunity for her to really get close to me, the way she had always longed to be. The staff lady said, "OK, but I'm not sure how." As we spoke, an amazing thing happened. Renee started scooting herself over towards the wall, making room for me to get in bed with her! I was amazed that she was able to scoot herself over! And so quickly, too! The staff lady lowered the bed rail. I followed my Mom's hand signal to stand next to the long side of the little bed. Then, very slowly, but deliberately, my Mom pressed her shoulder into my shoulder, tipping me slowly until I was lying in bed next to Renee. For a brief moment, I lay there with my legs all stiffly stretched out in front of me. After all, I had just been taken off my feet. It was strange to me. Something my Mom had never done to me before. But then I realized I was secure and wouldn't fall and as I felt Renee's hand gently stroke the side of my face, I relaxed my whole body. My legs dangled loosely from the side of the little bed. My Mom told me later that Renee smiled from ear to ear like we had never seen her smile before. I must have spent about 30 minutes that day lying with her. We were about the same height from head to toe lying next to each other in that little bed. She kissed me sweetly on the top of my head more times than I could count and between kisses she smiled and stroked my side. The two of us were blissfully happy snuggling there together. We both closed our eyes and savored the moment.

After that day, the staff members would always ask Renee if she wanted to lie on a mat with me in the living room. It was difficult for her to be placed on the mat on the floor and then lifted up into her wheelchair afterwards, but she and I had many snuggles there on the mat together.

Chapter 13
The Ideal Therapist

The Rehabilitation Therapist, or RT, supervising the therapy session has the authority to create an atmosphere in which the most effective interactions between the people and the dogs has the opportunity to take place. If the RT is a dog lover, that is a very good start. The RT will set the tone for the session by his/her affection for the therapy dogs. In between patients, I spend time with each staff member in the room. Working in a hospital can be quite stressful, so I take time to help the staff manage their day by relaxing with me a minute too.

The ideal therapist supervises and corrects the behavior of the patients if they are too rough or abrupt with the dogs. If the patient is unwilling to modify their conduct, the therapist would have to remove them from the session.

When a patient is petting me, it is best if they are the only person touching me. That way I can relate to them more fully, without distraction. I "read" the person, sensing what they need from me. I remember one day on Sub Acute when I witnessed a vivid example of this. My co-worker, Mischa, a Toy Poodle, was on a patient's bed. I was waiting my turn, so I had the opportunity to stand by and watch. The adult male patient was very frail, and was stroking Mischa very, very slowly. In an effort to show the patient that the dog was friendly, the RT herself, was also patting the small dog. Since it was Mischa's first day on the job, her owner was inexperienced and was probably not even aware of the fact that she, too, was patting him. Three adult human hands were all patting the 7 pound dog at once! My Mom, watched for a moment and then knew what she must do. She stepped forward, and gently put her fingers around the RT's wrist. She slowly moved the RT's hand away from the dog. Seeing my Mom's correction, Mischa's owner followed suit. The instant there was only one person left petting him, you could see Mischa's body relax! Mischa breathed a sigh of relief and melted next to the man he had come to visit. Being touched by 3 people at once (for any dog) is too stimulating and sends conflicting messages to him. Of the 3 people, he naturally loves his owner the most, but figures he should pay attention to the bedridden man. It's much too confusing for the dog.

Sometimes there are 20 or more people in a large room waiting for the session with the dogs to begin. In cases such as that, the patients should be assembled in the room *before* the dogs come in. It's unnerving for the dogs to have many people descend upon them if the dogs are in the room first and then the patients walk in or are wheeled in.

In a facility where the dogs will be taken from room to room to visit the patients, the RT should compile a list of room numbers of the patients who want to see the dogs, before the dogs arrive. This eliminates wasted time during the hour the dogs are on the unit.

Even when I'm not shedding, a few of my white hairs will still be left on people. Most folk don't mind this at all, but for those who do, the RT can have a clothing brush available at the end of the session. Some people are very annoyed at getting even one hair on them while the person next to them is petting me. Our intention is not to annoy anyone, so a clothing brush can be used.

The ideal therapist takes notes during or after the session, remarking on changes he/she sees in the patients. They also give the dog owners feedback from time to time when something truly remarkable happens with a patient. Not knowing the person's history, the dog owner will not understand the fullness of the benefit the therapist has witnessed unless they are told about it. Any conversation about the patients should take place OFF the unit, out of the range of hearing of any patients, *not* in the hallway between rooms. It has given us such joy to be told that a patient has smiled for the first time in weeks when the dog licked her finger. We've also been told of breakthroughs. Like the time when a person who had not spoken since being admitted to the psychiatric unit cried and cried while cuddling a Sheltie named Topper, and then after the session spoke openly with the Psychiatrist about what had been bottled up inside her. Knowing about these little miracles is an encouragement to the volunteers who bring their dogs and really warms their hearts.

The ideal therapist also remembers my favorite 'kissy spot' on my forehead and indulges me from time to time.

Chapter 14
Strengthening the Weak

Starting work at a new ward in a hospital or a new facility is always intriguing to me because I may be asked to do special things for the patients. On my first day on the job at a physical rehabilitation ward at a hospital, my two co-workers and I entered a large gym with our owners. The room was decorated with brightly colored games and exercise equipment for the patients to use. I saw a colorful nerf ball/Velcro dart board, shiny stainless steel hand rails to assist patients learning to walk again, and king sized mats on elevating devices which the patients used to exercise.

The patients on this unit are recovering from a variety of things such as strokes, spinal cord injuries, hip replacement or head injuries. Their goal is to get back to functioning in everyday life at home. I found this to be a very positive environment where after a sometimes long recovery, going home is within sight. The patients practice cooking, making a bed, and even gardening.

The Rehab Therapist (RT) in charge asked me to stand in one place while a male patient slowly walked over to me. Petting me was going to be his reward for making the effort to walk all that way. His feet thumped as he walked stiffly. A strong Physical Therapist (PT) held him up as he struggled to make every step. After successfully walking about 8 steps, he finally arrived at me ... well, almost at me. My Mom took to heart the effort the man had exerted to get that far, and in her compassion asked the PT if I would be allowed to move the one more step needed for the man to touch me. The PT nodded. The man had worked very hard and had done a great job. Mom tapped me on the chest twice with her hand and

43

said, "back". I took one step backwards where I ended up right in front of the man. His hand fumbled in my fur. He smiled. The height of my back came just below the man's hip, so he could easily reach me to pet me on my head and back. The man relaxed somewhat after the effort of his long journey and while the PT continued to steady his balance, he stood and patted me for a few minutes. From time to time Mom whispered "stand" to me to remind me to keep all of my weight on all fours and not to lean on the man's legs. That could have knocked him over.

Another male patient there that day made a significant breakthrough. As he was standing and petting me, the RT who was helping hold him steady said something about me being big enough for her to ride. (I get told that a lot.) The patient started giggling at the idea of her riding me. He ended up laughing out loud so hard that he found it difficult to even get his words out anymore. He kept laughing and saying things like, "Yes. I'd like to see you riding around the room on this dog." After the session, the Rehab Therapist told us that this man had "only presented with a flat face" until then! He had been completely expressionless before that day, but he found a reason to smile again. When we passed his room about 30 minutes later, he waved his hand from his wheelchair and smiled another beautiful, big smile at me.

Chapter 15
In The Zone

Any dog lover we visit can tell when a therapy dog is really enjoying his/her work. Itsey Bitsey is an example of a therapy dog who took to her job from the very first day. She is a 9 pound Mini Poodle so she's small enough to be placed on a bed with a patient. She was somewhat stiff on the first bed on which she was placed, but from the *second bed* of her career as a therapy dog, Itsey was "in the zone". Her little body was completely relaxed, her eyes were half closed, with a look of serenity on her face. Usually it takes a new dog at least 2 or 3 trips to a facility to get the hang of what they're there to do and to be able to relax and enjoy themselves.

My Mom was talking with Itsey Bitsey's Mom after she had finished her hour on an adult oncology unit. The benefits to the patients there include emotional comfort, relief from boredom, and a distraction from pain and anxiety. Although somewhat tired after the hour spent giving of herself, Itsey was quite content.

Itsey's Mom said that when her gardener heard about Itsey's job at the hospital, he said he was so happy about the kindness that they were going to show to the hospital-bound people, that he wanted to do a kindness back to her. He said, "I'll plant your flowers for free this year!" What a beautiful gift. Every bloom will be a reminder of another patient's smile.

Chapter 16
Sprucing Up

This is *not* my favorite part of being a therapy dog. In fact, I'd just as soon be a "stinky dog" instead, but there aren't too many job openings for them. So I'll tell you some of my beauty secrets and what it takes to get ready to go.

Once a week, I get my nails filed and my ears cleaned. Mom and Dad have tried a variety of ways to do my nails, and I haven't been fond of any of them. If one of the other dogs is before me in line that day, I go hide in my housey and pretend I'm sleeping so maybe they'll forget to do my nails that week. They have used nail clippers, an electric grinder and an assortment of nail files. I hate them all! Nail clippers have to be the worst! The sound they make scares me, so I moan and wail just like I did when they started doing this when I was 3 months of age. Mom and Dad think it's funny because my wailing starts while she's still just *looking at* my foot. The only good thing about the clippers is that they're fast. Dad and I lay on the living room carpet. Dad's job is to restrain me if I get feisty. Sometimes, while Mom's clipping the nails on one of my back feet, I plant the other back foot in the center of her chest and then PUSH. This sends her rolling backwards and I get a moment's reprieve. Most of the time I lay quietly for the file, so that's why they do my nails once a week so there's not too much to file. Mom uses a coarse metal file to flatten my nails to an attractive length. Then she uses a fine metal file to smooth all of the edges. If you are more co-operative than I am for the clippers, you probably will only have to have your nails clipped and filed smooth once every 3 weeks.

I'm not the kind of guy who likes to take a bath, but I know that the next day I'll be going to work and that's really fun. Unlike the nail ordeal, I tolerate getting wet and scrubbed in quiet submission. My Mom and Dad give me a bath at home on the ranch. Getting me wet all the way to the skin takes a lot of water because I have a thick double coat. They use puppy shampoo on my face so it doesn't sting my eyes, and a natural whitening shampoo on the rest of my body so that my coat comes up silvery white and soft. I like it when

Mom snuggles my head in a fluffy towel to dry it after she has washed and rinsed my face and ears. After my whole body has been washed and rinsed, I am walked around outside in the southern California sunshine for about 30 minutes on the leash. Then it's inside the house to sleep in my housey and air dry.

On the day that I am going to work, Mom brings me inside the house and locks the doggie door for about 2 hours before we are scheduled to leave the house. That way she'll know that I have not gone potty for the past two hours, and will give me the opportunity right before we get into the car. If the doggie door was not locked for that period of time, Mom wouldn't know whether I had *just gone* potty or whether I was just *thinking about* going outside when she puts the leash on me to take me to the car. I am not given any food to eat for at least 2 hours before leaving the house. Who would want to pet a dog with food stuck in his teeth?

I am brushed thoroughly from head to toe, including my hairy feet. It's important to brush down deep into my coat to remove any small mats forming, not just on the surface of the fur. It feels really good to be brushed, and afterwards, I like how the air can move through my fur.

If it's a work day *between* my scheduled baths, Mom brushes me thoroughly and then sprinkles a little baby powder on me. She rubs the baby powder into my coat well, and then brushes it out. This makes me smell fresh but not perfumed and it whitens the areas that need whitening. It also removes any excess oils on the hair.

She smells my ears, and if necessary, cleans them with a little rubbing alcohol on a cotton ball. She smells my breath, and if needed, brushes my teeth and sprays a squirt of doggie breath spray in my mouth. She looks under my tail (*just* looks) and makes sure my fur is clean.

Then I'm completely ready to go to work. I take a nap for about an hour while Mom gets ready. I'll skip the details about what she does to get herself ready, but she ends up dressed in clean, casual clothes. She wears close-toed, lace-up shoes so that she won't loose her balance or slip on the hospital floors. She never wears perfume to take me to work because it could be nauseating to the patients. She takes special care to wash her hands and scrub her nails just before leaving home.

Then when she's completely ready, she makes sure that her excitement and anticipation are under control. After having seen so many wonderful things happen in the sessions with the therapy dogs, Mom has come to expect it. This anticipation can make her tummy do some flip flops and she has even been so excited that she has been trembling. But she cannot get me out of my housey in that state because her nervousness would transfer to me. I would then be worried about what's wrong with Mom instead of doing my best work. So Mom sits on the edge of her bed and prays that God give her His peace in her body and mind. When she's completely quiet within herself, she goes to get my leash.

Another method an owner can use which may sound funny, but works well, is if the owner imagines they are waiting for a bus . . . a bus that's very late. They take on the demeanor of boredom and that works well to quiet their excitement.

Mom puts my rolled leather working collar on me and clips on my 6 foot nylon leash. If the two of us were just going on an outing to a coffee shop patio or somewhere, she'd put my usual nylon choke collar on me with my 6 foot nylon leash. But to go to work, I wear a collar that won't tighten around my neck. This is for my comfort in the facility and to avoid such an occasion that a patient might accidentally (or on purpose) pull the loop on my collar to tighten it around my neck. A therapy dog should walk politely by his handler's side, so a flexi leash or retractable leash is not appropriate, even if it is locked to a short length. We dogs can recognize a flexi leash when it's clipped onto our collar and it tells us that we're allowed to roam around or lead our owner on a walk. A flexi leash teaches a dog to pull away from his/her owner. This is not the way a therapy dog should walk while he/she is working. So instead, I wear my regular 6 foot leash.

Then the trick is to get out the front door without Kasheena following along. She sees the collar and leash being put on me and she wants to go to work too. She tries to squeeze her way out the front door, but Mom has to tell her "out" and she walks away sadly from the doorway and lets us leave the house. Sometimes she and I work together at a facility. It's great when we both get to go. Of course Dad comes along too when Kasheena comes with us. Only one dog per handler. It's not recommended for one handler to try to watch two dogs *and* two patients. A person just doesn't have enough eyes to do all that. And having two dogs right next to each other diverts the attention of the dogs from the people to each other.

Once outside, Mom leads me, on leash, to one of my favorite potty places and points the signal and tells me, "go pee pee". I do. She tells me I'm a good boy and we get into the van.

On the way to the facility, Mom always remembers to say a prayer. She asks God to love His people through the dogs. And she prays that the dogs and handlers behave appropriately and be led by Him.

When we arrive at the facility, Mom takes me to a tree of her choice, far away from the front door of the building. She points to the tree, giving the hand signal while she says, "go pee pee". I either do or don't, but I know that this is my only chance until after the hour. No other tree will be sniffed or selected. After giving me about a minute to sniff the tree from all sides, if I haven't gone potty it's because I don't need to. Mom tells me "leave it" and gives the "leave it" hand signal. That tells me the potty window of opportunity is closed until further notice.

Yippee! Now it's time to enter the building and go see some old friends and make some new ones! This makes all the preparation suddenly worthwhile! Mom tells me "work" in a happy voice, and in we go.

Chapter 17
A Few Pointers

If you're just starting work as a therapy dog and your owner is new to taking you to work, I have a few tips that will help you both.

If you're working with a dog you've never met before, have your owner and the other dog's owner each "heel" you back and forth in the parking lot, eventually passing by each other about 2 feet apart. Keep your attention on your owner, and do your best to ignore the other dog. If the two of you will be working in a session where you will probably brush by each other, then practice this in the parking lot too. Walk past each other in opposite directions and then stop when you are side to side so that you can feel his/her fur touch the side of your body. Your faces will be at opposite ends, and you still won't sniff each other. If you try to sniff the other dog, your owner can say "manners" to tell you to stop. It sometimes embarrasses the patients if dogs sniff each other, so you should each act like professionals and keep your mind on your work. Some dog owners think the dogs should be allowed to play together in the parking lot before going on the unit. I disagree because it makes it difficult for the dogs to switch from silly antics to serious work. Play is best done another day.

If a patient takes one look at you and says, "Why can't you bring a cat?", don't take it personally.

If you're a big dog (like me), and someone says, "I like little dogs." don't take offense at that either. Your owner should just smile and say "OK" or "Have a nice day." and move on to another person. Don't try to change the person's mind.

When your owner walks up to the patient to greet them, he/she should not say, "How are you?". The answer might use up your whole hour. Now, I'm not saying my Mom doesn't talk with patients and form some relationships after visiting some of the same people year after year, but that is the exception, not the norm. For the most part, she'll greet a patient with, "Hello. Breeze is here to see you." or "Hello. Would you like to pet the dog?" or "Look who came to see you today." It is a wonderful thing when people go to nursing homes or hospitals to talk with the residents, but that's *not* Animal Assisted Therapy. In AAT, it's the *dog* that visits with the patient, not the owner. And how the patients look forward to their time with the dogs!

If a little lady in a nursing home saves you the chicken out of her lunch, don't accept it. She needs it more than you do. Your mouth is probably watering at the thought of it, which shows you that food treats distract a therapy dog from visiting with the person. Instead, they're just looking for another treat. Your owner can say, "He only eats dog food.". My Mom got a bit soft on this point when the little lady with the slice of chicken in her hand looked disappointed, so the next time we came to visit, Mom brought one of my dog biscuits from home and gave it to the lady to feed to me. Mom thought that would make the lady happy, and it did, but for the rest of the hour I had one thing on my mind: "Do you have a treat?" If I didn't smell a treat, then one whiff later I was on to the next person. Not much therapy work was done that day. So save the treats for at home, or if you must, in the car after the hour is done. Some handlers think that a food treat should be given to the dog in the hallway between patient rooms. This is actually counter productive and encourages the dog to rush through the visit with the patient in order to get back into the hallway where he/she will be rewarded with food. Dogs should be rewarded with praise, not food, during their hour of work. After all, if the petting was not the reward, the dog would not be doing this work. A good therapy dog will never be in it "for the food". He/she has to love to be petted and talked to. *That's* what motivates them to visit strangers.

If a strong patient has one of you little dogs held tightly in his arms and won't let go of you, don't panic. Stay still and have your owner tell the patient that you have to go outside to "potty". That usually does the trick.

If you or your owner are not feeling well, call in sick, and stay home. Your good hearted intentions of keeping your scheduled visit is commendable, but the people there should not be exposed to colds or flu germs.

If you have open wounds or hot spots, stay home.

If you're a girl dog who's not spayed, you should stay home if you're in season.

If you're a boy dog, you should never "mark" the wall inside a hospital. You and your owner should walk down the middle of the hallway, thus eliminating any possibility of male marking. Some boys can lift a leg and mark a wall so fast, without even losing step! Boys with a problem in this area should not start work as a therapy dog until they have overcome this behavior through training. They should also learn to urinate on command when on leash. If your owner doesn't want to be quite as graphic as the command my Mom uses, he/she could use "hurry up" or "get busy" instead.

If you see a pill on the floor, don't eat it. Your owner will be checking the floor for your safety as you move throughout the facility. Also, you should never stick your head under a bed or in a trash can. You might find some nasty surprises there, such as soiled tissues or dressings.

If you see a tray table next to the side of a patient's bed, don't go to the *opposite* side of the bed for them to pet you, thinking there's more room there. The tray table is on that side because that is the hand that is stronger and able to pet you. Slowly move the tray table aside, stand in it's place, and repeat to yourself "Put the tray table back. Put the tray table back." until you do so at the end of your visit.

And lastly, if you're with a patient and they're really enjoying being with you, don't rush to go on to the next patient. Relax and enjoy them. Your goal should not be to touch every person in a facility, but rather, to touch those you do, deeply.

Chapter 18
Don't Go It Alone

So if you're wondering, "Can I be a therapy dog?" here's what you need to consider: Do I enjoy being petted by strangers? Am I calm, confident and well mannered? Am I tolerant of unusual noises and being in new places? If you answer "yes" to these questions, then you are an excellent candidate for therapy work. If you answered "yes" to some of these questions, but not all, and it's in your heart to do this work, then get in touch with a dog trainer who uses positive reinforcement. With effort and the correct method, the "nos" can change to "yeses".

Have your owner contact your local S.P.C.A. or veterinarian for referrals to groups already established in your area. You can also go on-line and search under therapy dogs or Animal Assisted Therapy. You will discover that different groups visit various types of facilities and the requirements and testing will vary from group to group. Some groups might want you to "entertain" patients, more than giving cuddles. Study and compare and then make your selection.

Don't start visiting facilities without joining a group. By being part of a local or national organization you'll be temperament tested and guided through the proper channels to really work as a certified therapy dog. You will also be covered by the group's insurance policy. You'll likely be given a scarf or badge to wear so everyone you meet in a facility will know you're a therapy dog.

Chapter 19
The Test

Although you will be eager to do your best when you go to be evaluated and temperament tested, don't be nervous. Your owner must be relaxed also or it may cause you to behave badly.

The testing you undergo will vary widely from group to group. The objective of this chapter is to give you some idea of what you might experience during the test. The tester will be identifying your strengths and taking note of commands that you obey. For example, a skill such as a reliable "down - stay" may allow you to work with more critically ill patients. If you will obey hand signals in addition to voice commands, this will also be noted. These things, together with your level of confidence and trust in your owner, will show the tester in which type of facility you will be best suited to work.

Your owner should know and recognize signs of job stress such as profuse shedding, a wet mouth, or a refusal to follow a command. If you encounter a situation when you are working as a therapy dog which triggers one of these (or some other indicator that you are upset) your owner must be able to spot it. One time, a patient was scratching my back and accidentally broke the skin with a sharp finger nail. I have so much thick fur that Mom could not see the small cut, but she saw the saliva well up in my usually dry mouth. She took me out of the session for about 5 minutes to examine me and sit quietly with me. Although she did not find the cause until she felt the scab the next day, the time she spent with me allowed me to recover from the trauma and return to normal so that I could go back into the session and finish the hour.

An important test of a good therapy dog is how the dog responds when someone *stops* petting him/her. It is desirable for the dog to place his/her face gently on the patient's knee or to *gently* nudge the patient's hand with his/her nose to ask for more petting. It is also passable for the dog to walk away in acceptance. However, it is NOT acceptable for the dog to paw the patient's arm or jump up and clobber the person when the petting stops. Such a dog needs more training before he/she can be a therapy dog.

These are the items usually tested:

1. Do you allow the stranger (tester) to shake hands with your owner without growling or jumping up to demand to be petted.
2. Do you accept the stranger's petting without shying or backing away?
3. Will you sit politely for petting?
4. How do you react when the tester *stops* petting you?
5. Are your coat and nails well groomed?
6. Will you walk by your owner's side without pulling ahead?
7. Can you reasonably ignore other dogs who are 3 feet away from you or are you driven to either play with them or fight with them?
8. How do you react to a sudden, loud noise in the room? How long does it take for you to recover?
9. Are you afraid of a walker or a wheelchair?
10. Will you tolerate clumsy petting?
11. Will you tolerate a restraining hug by your owner?
12. If you are a small dog, will you allow your owner to pick you up to be placed on a bed or chair?
13. How do you act when your owner is asked to leave the room and you are left with the tester holding your leash? Do you trust that your owner will come back?
14. Do you know any tricks?

If you will be working with children, you will likely undergo additional testing. While you lay down next to the adult tester sitting on the floor, he/she may evaluate you on the following:

1. Pinching your toes and/or holding your foot
2. Gently pulling your leg
3. Poking you around your body with a finger
4. Fiddling with your ears and mouth
5. Your reaction to a sudden movement
6. Your acceptance of being hugged and/or kissed by the tester
7. Your reaction when the tester bursts into tears and/or squeals
8. Your reaction to commotion from many children in the room

If you pass all of these items with flying colors, you will be re-tested with a child.

As I mentioned before, an important part of preparing for the test is to have your owner take you on outings to a variety of places where you are petted by strangers. Dogs are usually allowed in banks, hardware stores, coffee shop patios and other places.

Chapter 20
The Grand Scope of AAT

Animal Assisted Therapy has come a long way in the past 20 years. Today, therapy dogs, cats, birds, llamas, donkeys and other animals have been widely used to benefit patients all over the United States and other countries.

I remember another Great Pyrenees owner telling my Mom how she snuck her adult male Pyr into her son's hospital room years ago. The boy was hospitalized for several months following a head injury, and twice a week during that time she snuck his favorite doggie friend into his room. Back then dogs were not allowed into hospitals. The lady would put the dog on a "down - stay" on the lawn outside her son's room. Then she'd leave the dog there and go into the hospital through the front door, greeting the nurses along the way. When she got into her son's room, she'd open the window and say, "Blizzard, Come!" and Blizzard would jump through the open window! The dog would snuggle with his comatose friend week after week. The joyous day when her son began emerging from the coma, his first word was "Blizzard".

Today, thankfully, we don't have to sneak a 120 lb. dog in through an open window to visit people because now the proven, positive benefits of AAT have brought us to the point of being welcomed and invited into facilities. Being a therapy dog or a therapy dog owner carries an awesome responsibility. When we go into a facility, we represent therapy dogs everywhere, working through a multitude of large and small organizations. The good that we do reflects on the reputation of *all* therapy dogs.

Photo by Wendy Victor

63

Index

responsibility, 62

"shake" (see tricks), 21
sleeping dogs, 20
sniffing, 16, 53
"stand" command, 44
stopping petting, 60
stress in dog, 15, 59
sub-acute ward, 11-13

talking with patients, 54
testing, 59-61
tray table, 55
treats, food, 30, 54
tricks, 21-22
tricks with ears, 22
tricks, barking in, 22

violent patients, 19

wheelchair, positioning dog, 16

About the Author

Lorna Stanart has had 8 years of experience as the owner and handler of certified therapy dogs. She was a volunteer with Delta Society for 3 years of service with her mixed breed dog, a Terrier/ Whippet named Rex. During those 3 years, Rex and Lorna visited psychiatric facilities and long-term hospital wards. To date, Breeze and Lorna have been working as a team for 5 years.

She is currently serving in two capacities with Animal Samaritans SPCA Inc. As Director of Orientations she helps screen and temperament test new dogs wanting to join the program. Her job of Hospital Coordinator requires that she place and supervise the dogs who are working in several hospital wards and psychiatric facilities. She has held both of these positions for 3 years.

Lorna has been interviewed and quoted on several occasions in newspaper articles about therapy dogs and in news segments shot on location at hospitals and nursing homes.

Lorna has had animals all her life. She has a sensitivity to what an animal is saying through its body language. She enjoys matching each new therapy dog to the type of facility in which it will be best suited to work.

You can e-mail Lorna at HispenBooks@aol.com